CONFESSIONS
OF A TWO-TIMER

CONFESSIONS
OF A TWO-TIMER

ELEVEN GAMES WITH AN ORDINARY KITCHEN
TIMER TO FIND FLOW, OVERCOME
PROCRASTINATION, WIN PRIZES, BE POPULAR
AND BECOME A NEIGHBORHOOD BUDDHA

BEAR JACK GEBHARDT

Senior Librarian, Heart Mountain Monastery

Published by Seven Traditions Press
Bellvue, CO   London, UK   Singapore   Des Moines, IA.

This goofy little book is

dedicated to Suzy,

loving wife of a hundred years, who loaned me her timer, and who makes every moment a heaven on earth, and with whom I intend to spend eternity.

Table of Contents

Table of Contents (Cont.)

Why I Wrote This Little Book

"We have failed to recognize our great assett: time. A conscientious use of it could make us into something quite amazing." --Friedrick Schiller

I wrote this book because after years of successfully experimenting with an ordinary kitchen timer in (almost) all areas of my life, it became clear that such a book could be quite timely (so to speak) for a wider audience. You'll know if it's right for you in just a *second..* Oh, wait a *minute . . .*

Experimenting with a kitchen timer?

Yes. Here's why:

For most of my life, like almost everyone else, I have basically been experimenting, sometimes methodically, most often quite randomly, with how to experience more peace, more prosperity, more love, more flow and good humor, e.g., how to be more awake, more lively, more present in my daily walk-around world. The experiments have not always been successful.

Warning to Americans and Japanese: Fifty or sixty or eighty hour work weeks do _not_ lead to more peace, more prosperity, more love and good humor in our lives. I know because I tried this experiment in at least half a dozen different rough seasons throughout my life. And many of my friends tried it too. We have repeatedly proven that a fifty to eighty hour work week _never_ generates more peace, more love and good humor.

What _does_ work, surprisingly, is a little five-dollar kitchen timer. Along with a somewhat monkish, or nunnish view of life.

I am a householder monk at Heart Mountain Monastery, Nunnery and Art Colony, which is a Taoist-Budhist-Quaker-Methodist online/offline community of old and new friends, pilgrims and fellow travelers. (I'm just now coming out of the closet about my monkish predilection).

I often use a simple kitchen timer, which I carry in a home-made holster on my hip, because I've found the timer helps me, at least a little, to not procrastinate so much, and be more present to the mystery of life, inside and out. My timer also helps me be more alert, and thus more grateful. It also helps me to not be so regularly kidnapped by what the existentialist philosopher Colin Wilson called "the robot mind."

I wrote this book to share my surprise, and the discoveries I've made with the kitchen timer. In brief: I sleep better, my finances are better, my love life is divine, my professional accomplishiments are increasingly satisfying and the kitchen itself generally remains more tidy.

All due to my use of the kitchen timer?

Well, a few other factors that we'll talk about were also involved. But my little five-dollar kitchen timer functions time and time again (*heh-heh*), as grease for the wheels, rudder for the ship. It has been my faithful companion, my tireless, uncomplaining miniature workhorse, my secret friend. It deserves wider recognition. This little book is my "thank you" to my uncomplaining, ever-faithful little kitchen timer buddy.

P.S. I've learned to use and enjoy my timer so much that I have many timers stashed in different places around my house. I don't always have my timer-holster on my belt. Thus, ***I'm a two-timer***!

(Actually, I'm not going to confess how many timers I own. I'll just admit that I am *at least* a two-timer!)

WHY YOU SHOULD READ THIS BOOK

Question: *How many people with Attention Deficit Disorder does it take to change a light bulb?*

Answer: *Want to go ride bikes?*

*W*ith a few rare exceptions, we *all* have attention deficit disorder, to one degree or another. And no wonder! According to the latest neurological research, our senses are bombarded with over **11 million bits of data every SECOND**. (Repeat: 11 MILLION bits every SECOND!)

The average person's working memory can handle 40-50 bits, max. That means we must (and do) ignore 10,999,950 bits of data every second we are awake. How do we decide what to ignore, and what not?

For example, I start to do the dishes but as I clear the counter my attention gets caught by a magazine. I glance through it quickly. As I do so, a car advertisement reminds me I need to call cousin Louie about driving to the game. So I put the magazine down to go look up Louie's phone number and then suddenly remember that in his last e-mail Louie announced he'd changed his phone number. So now to call Louie I need to quickly look at his last e-mail, so I go to my computer, open my e-mail and then ...

Yea, right. An hour later I hear my wife in the kitchen doing the dishes. Yikes! I jump up. It was my turn! Not that I didn't think about doing the dishes during that hour but something else had caught my attention, something else was more fun, "just for a minute..."

If I had set my timer, the dishes would be done.

A timer is a way of managing attention. The timer itself is not magical, but *attention* is. "What you put your attention on, grows." As a practicing monk, I want to decide where I put my attention, and where I don't, on a regular basis.

You don't need to be a monk or a nun to experience the advantages of a timer, and consciously deciding where to put your attention. This book shares not only very specific and useful tips on how to use a timer in both work and play, but more important it explores *why* a timer—playing the Timer Game — works so well to bring *flow* into our lives, peace to our minds, prosperity to our circumstances.

Timer Game = *Play* Time!

Once you know the *why* behind the use of a timer, you'll start inventing your own personal uses, tricks and tips. I'd love to hear about them. Feel free to contact me at:

bear @heartmountainmonastery.com

So the first couple of chapters are designed to lay the ground- work for *why* we play the Timer Game, and what it's about. Later chapters then give specific areas, specific "fields" where playing the Timer Game is most useful. You are not, of course, obliged to read the first essays in the book. (As you know, you aren't obliged to read ANY of this book.) But the timer "theory," or philosophy helps put the game into a wider context, such that when it comes time (!) to play the game itself, you'll more often give yourself permission to pick up the timer. The intent of the book is to encourage you to actually try it yourself, play the Timer Game , and then let me know your experience. So without further delay. . .

CHAPTER 1.
THE TIMER GAMES MEAN _PLAY_ TIME!

"What man needs most of all is a game worth playing."
---Robert De Roppe, _The Master Game_

As mentioned, playing with a kitchen timer is a _game_ I play off and on throughout the day to help me experience more flow, more peace of mind, more productivity and less procrastination. But as with any game, it should be fun.

WARNING: USING YOUR TIMER SHOULD _ALWAYS_ BE FUN. **IF IT'S NOT FUN, DON'T DO IT!**

In 1938 Dutch linguist, Johan Huizinga, published a little book, which has since become a classic, entitled _Homo Ludens_. The thesis of his book is that we human beings **are not** basically _homo sapiens_—the logical, reasoning beings—but rather, _homo ludens_—the beings who play, or make up games. Looking at where we so often secretly put our attention, "_homo ludens_" makes sense, yes?

The mass popularity of football, basketball, baseball, golf, tennis, Jeopardy, The Bachelor and the ubiquitous government sponsored lotteries or "games of chance," along with computer games, solitaire and crossword puzzles would suggest Huizinga might be spot on.

However, Huizinga came from a fairly rigid, even uptight, old century, pre-war "Germanic" world view, in which game playing and plain old fun were apparently viewed quite skeptically. (Not unlike the world view of most of our current politicians, academics, economists and Church Bishops.)

Huizinga suggests a game must have five characteristics, but he forgot all about fun! *Fun* is the most important characteristic of any game. Huizinga defined the five characteristics with a distinct allegiance to the militaristic mood of his time. Nevertheless, his classic, somewhat stiff descriptions of what a game must entail are useful for seeing the wider context of the *Timer Game.* This chapter describes how the Timer Game fits, and does not fit Huizinga's "game criteria." Our sense of play continues to evolve. The game characteristics in bold are Huizinga's criteria. The italics are mine.

1. Play is free, is in fact freedom.

(The Timer Game is free, is in fact freedom itself.)

10

Timer Game = *Play* Time!

This one is right on. I *never* let myself feel obligated, or *forced* to use my timer. This is a game we play—or don't play—in response to our momentary mood. It is *always* our *free choice* to play or not play the Timer Game . We do it for fun, not because we should, or because it's good for us.

At a higher level, I've discovered, and various friends have confirmed, that when we use our timer, when we play the Timer Game , rather than feeling *bound* by time, as one might suspect, such play has the exact opposite effect: **the timer *frees* us from time!** At least a little.

The Timer Game helps us escape "the heavy hands of time" more easily and more frequently than almost any other game we can play! Paradoxical, yes, but, as we will see, quite understandable. In a nutshell: **when we let our timer tell time for us, watch the clock for us, *we don't have to*!** It's like having a personal assistant taking care of details.

2. Play is not "ordinary" or "real" life.

(The Timer Game is not for ordinary, or real life.)

Absolutely **NOT** true. The Timer Game fits *perfectly* in almost every aspect of our real, ordinary lives, whether you are a monk or a nun or a bus driver or disco dancer!

To suggest we should not play games (like the monk and nun game!) in our ordinary lives is true only if we accept, along with most of Western civilization, that ordinary life, real life comprises mostly work, woe, despair and drudgery. Apparently play was *not* part of ordinary life back just prior to World War 2 when Huizinga wrote his book. But consciousness has evolved since then.

I play—or have played— the Timer Game throughout almost *every* aspect of my ordinary life: cleaning the kitchen, mowing the lawn, preparing a report, doing the taxes. My experience is that this game lifts, at least a bit, the sense of burden, woe and drudgery so often associated with "ordinary, real life" such that I can (at least inwardly) whistle while I work.

As you will see when we get to more specific uses of the timer, the Timer Game functions as a wonderful adjunct to, and in support of, almost every aspect of our real, ordinary every day lives!

3. Play is distinct from "ordinary" life both as to locality and duration.

(The Timer Game is distinct from "ordinary" life both as to locality and duration.)

Timer Game = *Play* Time!

Again, absolutely not true. The Timer Game adds dimension and ambience to whatever we happen to be doing.

I have played the Timer Game in almost *every locality* in my ordinary life—at home, at work, at the store, even in the car. (I generally don't use the timer while on an airplane, as the sound of a timer going off tends to make other passengers very nervous.)

As far as duration, that's one of the real powers and beauties of playing the Timer Game . This game does indeed change—brighten and enlighten— the "duration" of various aspects of ordinary life, either giving a sense of time being stretched out while doing the things we enjoy, or time being shortened while doing the chore or project we don't enjoy so much. The Timer Game can add dimension and deliciousness to *any* aspect of ordinary life, from doing the dishes to weeding the garden to preparing the monthly job report.

4. Play creates order, is order. Play demands order absolute and supreme.

(The Timer Game creates order, is order. The Timer Game demands order absolute and supreme.)

Yes, indeed: the Timer Game is itself a way of bringing order, organization and flow back into our lives.

I'm not sure about "absolute and supreme, " (that doesn't sound like much fun) but as far as "the Timer Game creates order," Huizinga is *exactly* right relative to this game. For example, when I find myself with too many things on my to-do list (which in my relaxed, *sanyasi* maturity I have re-named my "*could-do*" list), and I am feeling a bit overwhelmed and/or burdened by all the demands made on my attention, I know it's time to once again re-engage the Timer Game . As we will see, one of the beautiful things about playing the Timer Game is that it allows us to focus just on the chore at hand, indeed, *enjoy* the chore at hand, while other chores and responsibilities wait patiently on the sidelines.

When Huizinga says that the game is "absolute and supreme," he is undoubtedly referring to the agreed upon boundaries and rules of various games. According to football rules, a player on the sidelines is not allowed to run onto the field and help his mates just because the opportunity presents itself. When playing scrabble, a player cannot simply make up a word and put it anywhere she wants on the board. "Game rules" and boundaries are necessary, "absolute and supreme," and not only make the game more fun, but make the game a *game*!

When it comes to the Timer Game , the only "absolute and supreme" rule is, as stated at the beginning of this chapter, **Using the timer should**

***always* be fun. If it's not fun, don't use it**. As a monk, I believe we human beings are constantly evolving to a higher state of consciousness. I believe the fundamental energy behind such evolution is joy, which is another word for love. **If we are enjoying our daily life games, we are evolving. If we are not enjoying our daily life games, we are devolving**. So again, enjoy your timer. Otherwise, don't use it.

5. Play is connected with no material interest, and no profit can be gained from it

(The Timer Game is connected with no material interest and no profit can be gained from it.)

Again, not true. Such a view of play is silly and simply not reflective of how we humans function.

Nevertheless, "no profit can be gained from play" was indeed the view of old-time religion, and old time industrialists, and for many of our present-day bosses!

My own experience is that the more often I am able to bring "play" into my material interests and profit-oriented activities, the more likely they are to be successful. (Yes, we monks and nuns, at least at Heart Mountain Monastery, still have material interests and profit oriented activities)

The hippie billionaire Richard Branson comes to mind. Starting with Virgin Records, and then Virgin Rail and Virgin Air, Sir Richard, with a grin on his face, seems to always have had a sense of fun, of "game playing," in his personal approach to building his business empires. It doesn't mean he's not serious about his businesses, or that he takes his responsibilities lightly. Rather, he's simply aware that this is his real life and it should be, or at least could be, fun, adventurous, *interesting*.

On a much more modest level, I've discovered the Timer Game brings more fun and adventure into my own daily material and profit oriented activities, as well as my spiritual (if we must make a distinction) and charitable activities.   Or at least, the Timer Game helps me not get stuck in the dead-end drudgery of such activities.

I've spent some time here putting the Timer Game into a broader context in order to show that what seems like a somewhat "trivial" little side-game can be, in fact, a very integral piece of "a life well-lived."   Or more simply, as Roald Dahl said, *"Life is more fun if you play games."*

Have I tweaked your interest in the Timer Game, and given you a broader context for why you might want to play it? I hope so.   Time to move on . . .

CHAPTER 2.

TAMING OUR PROMISCUOUS ATTENTION!

"The bad news is time flies. The good news is you're the pilot."--- Michael Althsuler

*T*he Timer Game is in essence a simple and powerful way of playing with our attention. More precisely, **the timer is a simple way for us to *frame* our attention**, with the result that time slows down (or speeds up, depending on what we want or need) and life gets big! Not only big, but easy. Or at least, easier.

I stumbled upon the Timer Game after many years of working in the addictions field with many hundreds of clients. Here in my silver-haired years, I've come to understand that *every* addiction is at root an addiction of attention.

It's our attention that first gets addicted, whether it be to gambling, sex, drugs, alcohol, movies, buying new shoes or running. This is a subtle yet powerful insight not yet widely emphasized in the field. (I've written many books about addiction, the latest being *The Smoker's Prayer. The Spiritual Healing of Tobacco Addiction with or without Chantix, Nicotine Patches, Hypnosis, Jail Time or Duct Tape.*)

In my addictions work, I recognized that since it is our *attention* that first becomes addicted, to get free, not only from addictions but from all sorts of suffering, we need to better understand and manage our attention. When our attention is free, we are free!

Attention is a magical energy. It's life's basic energy. **Whatever we put our attention on, grows**. Whether it be something positive or something negative, either way whatever we put our attention on will start to grow. Caring for our attention is a little like caring for a squirming, restless two-year-old—it's an ongoing, mandatory project. What a relief, then, when we find some game, or toy or safe environment that will keep the squirming two-year-old occupied for a while.

For most of us, our attention is almost uncontrollably promiscuous. We want our attention to be monogamous, and we often pretend that it is so, but our attention gets caught first here then there, and while it's in the middle of "there," something else catches it and off it goes. (Refer to my example of cleaning up the kitchen.)

Timer Game = *Play* Time!

First here, then there and everywhere, our attention is always on the move. We'd like to give it a rest. So maybe we turn on the television, or the computer game, or have a smoke. Or a bag of chips, something else to eat. Or we look for a crossword puzzle. And when we do, *ahh, yes. . .* our attention, for a brief minute, finds a little rest.

What we are doing with the television, the computer game, the crossword puzzle, etc. is ***framing our attention,*** if only unconsciously. We give it borders, boundaries, **a place to rest, not leave**, if only for a moment.

When we find some activity, or relationship, or drug or game in which our attention finds some joy, or even just a little rest, a little peace and relaxation, we tend to go back to it. It feels almost like a survival mechanism. **Our attention wants and needs this rest, this peace.**

And if on our return we again find a little rest or relief or pleasure—even if it's not as great as what we experienced the first time — that activity or relationship or game or drug will "catch" our attention. And again, what we put our attention on, grows.

So when we put our attention on that activity or relationship or game or drug, attention itself will "grow" that activity into our lives, to a point we become identified with it, e.g. addicted to it.

Okay, that's a brief overview of attention and the roots of addiction. Let's move on, with this caveat**: this *Timer Game* can be addictive!** I know this from personal experience. I'm now a timer junkie! (And my life's better for it!)

Here's how I got hooked: One of my early "eureka!" moments when it came to understanding the place and power of attention, and led to recognizing how it functions in the addiction process, was reading Michael Goldhaber's seminal essay, *"The Attention Economy, The Natural Economy of the Net."*

Reading his essay, I was reminded, again, how very valuable my attention was—is. Hard cash on the barrel-head valuable. **Our attention is something so familiar and commonplace that we often overlook its value**. But corporations are spending millions and millions of dollars every day to capture our normal every-day attention.

After reading Goldhaber's essay, I suddenly took the junk mail and billboards, television commercials and spam *personally*. I suddenly realized it was *my own personal attention* that all of these were aimed at capturing. I decided that since there were so many ruthless, unremitting, well-funded campaigns to capture my attention, all day, every day, for all manner of things, just to protect myself I needed to build up my "attention muscles."

At the time, I was commuting to work most every day to Boulder, Colorado, about forty miles from my home. So one day I took my wife's kitchen timer with the intention of training myself to "pay attention" during my commute. I was going to *really* pay attention to what was going on—out the windshield, and the side windows, and back windows. Look at everything really closely. I was going to train myself to really pay attention!

So I started by setting the timer for twenty minutes; my plan was to be *really alert* for just twenty minutes. Yeah, right. It never happened.

After trying several twenty minute trials, I got more real. "Okay. This time I'm going to try to *really pay attention* for just **two minutes**." Attention is indeed quite promiscuous.

Nevertheless, this was the start of my playing with the timer in relation to my attention. I discovered it was uniquely fun to really pay attention out the windshield for two minutes. With the timer going, whenever I noticed I was once again lost in some story in my head, I could drop the story and come back to paying attention to the drive. I had **made a decision as to**

where to put my attention! It was no longer haphazard.

Of course, I soon grew bored with putting my attention on the scenery. I realized I could use the timer to put my attention on some particular inner story, or idea, again for just two minutes or so. I was still a beginner. When my attention wandered to some different story, I would gently bring it back. I found this "attention discipline" was doable if I did it for a short period of time, just a couple of minutes, using the timer.

In brief, I discovered that the five-dollar portable kitchen timer is a very efficient tool for "framing" attention. And more precisely, for *reclaiming* attention, when necessary, from all of the random and promiscuous adventures it tends to engage. And most miraculous of all, I discovered that when I *intentionally* reclaim my attention, using the timer, I am able to **rest** my attention, be it on something as mundane as doing the dishes or as profound as how to experience more peace in my life.

IT IS THE DECISION ABOUT *WHAT* TO PAY ATTENTION TO THAT FIRST FRAMES ATTENTION. THE DECISION ABOUT HOW MUCH **TIME** TO DEVOTE REINFORCES THAT FRAME. Curiously, it's the reinforced frame that allows attention to rest more fully, enjoy more fully.

Timer Game = *Play* Time!

Now I use the timer a lot, most every day, primarily because it's fun and I enjoy it, but also because I find the timer helps me get the things done that I want to get done, or need to get done, while keeping my "get-high" mindset as I'm doing such things. (See my book, *The Potless Pot High: How to Get high, Clear and Spunky without Weed.*)

For example, back to the dishes. I will often look at the dishes and estimate that it will take me, say, twenty minutes to get the job done. So I set the timer for twenty minutes. Then, curiously, **when I'm doing the dishes, I'm just doing the dishes**! I'm not thinking about cousin Louie, or my e-mail, or maybe I should next do the laundry. I find when I set the timer for such an ordinary task, I am much more present, more relaxed, more willing to be here in the moment just doing what I'm doing. ("Chopping wood, carrying water," as the Zen folks might say.)

In business, deciding on a particular focus is called the "cost of opportunity." If I decide I'm going to make widgets, then I have lost the opportunity to make buggy whips. If I decide I'm going to do the dishes, I'm not cleaning the upstairs bathroom. Doesn't mean I won't at some time clean the upstairs bathroom or make buggy whips, but I don't need to put my attention there in this moment. **The timer helps me rest my attention on just what I'm doing**.

Here's an important part of this: Be clear that *I'm not trying to get the dishes done in twenty minutes.* Twenty minutes is just my estimate of how long this particular task will naturally, easily, take. I am not interested in adding more stress or pressure to my life. *Au contraire.* If it takes me 25 minutes to clean the kitchen, so be it. If I get it done in 15 minutes, that's okay too. **The purpose of using the timer is to *frame attention*** and more precisely **to rest attention**, free up attention to *just do the dishes*!

We make hundreds, even thousands of decisions a day as to what we will do next—take a shower, get dressed, do the dishes, do the taxes, mow the lawn, etc. My discovery was that when I "freeze framed" some of those tasks by using the timer, I slowed down, I was happier, I was more present, I had given myself permission to use my time in this way—I was not just "getting things done." I was enjoying my life as it was being lived!

Here's another important piece of this game. I've discovered that **actually using a <u>timer</u> is necessary— rather than trying to use a clock.** With a clock, I'm forced to constantly check the time, and remember when I started and when I'm supposed to stop. **With the timer, I can forget about time**!

Curiously, although it seems as though the timer makes us more conscious of time, it's one of the few

Timer Game = *Play* Time!

ways I know of that actually allows us, or more precisely, allows our attention, to escape time, to step outside of time. If we use a clock, we are forced to become clock watchers. Using a timer, we have a little servant who does that for us!

Although on the surface this appears to be a very "materialistic" game—you actually need to purchase and use a portable timer to play the Timer Game—I know from experience and with sharing the game with family, friends and clients that the use of a timer often turns out to be a very emotionally and psychologically centering practice. And yes, a somewhat addictive practice.

Once you catch on, you will undoubtedly discover hundreds of other personal uses for your timer. To get you started, in the following chapters I share eleven different uses of the timer—eleven different games— that I've discovered can be quite fun and useful. I encourage people to approach the timer games as different experiments, testing which ones are fun for them, which ones not, which ones help them giggle, which ones don't! In the next chapters you'll discover my starter pack.

Chapter 3

THE DAVID AND GOLIATH GAME
GAME 1: USE THE TIMER TO START A HUGE PROJECT

"Mountains cannot be surmounted except by winding paths."   ---Goethe

A good friend—a bright, retired school teacher—recently mentioned she was proud of herself for having just completed a large, overdue project. A large drawer in her den had been collecting junk for ten years or more. Whenever she had a photo or scrap of paper or some "maybe useful item" that she didn't know what to do with, she would toss it into that drawer to be "sorted out later."

"I decided it was time to clean out that drawer," she said. "So I just sat down and did it. "

"How long did it take?" I asked.

"All day. About eight hours," she said. "I stopped for lunch, of course. But I just stayed with it. It feels so good to have it done."

Good for her. We all occasionally find the time, place and motivation to devote ourselves to long overdue projects. But I would suggest that my friend's "drawer cleaning" project is an admirable exception to the general "rule of behavior" that we human beings engage. How many of us can or will devote a full day to clearing out a single drawer? How many of us feel we have eight hours "free" to devote to such a chore? (My friend is retired and lives alone.)

We all have huge projects that we don't want to start simply because, well, they're huge! We realize they could take eight hours, or eight days, eight months, and we don't have eight hours, or days! Or we simply don't feel like devoting eight hours.

Yes, we need to clean out the garage, or the attic, start on that woodpile, or that novel, or the taxes from two years ago. But the project is just *too huge* to even begin! We feel we don't have the time or the psychic energy.

We don't need to do the whole Huge Project at once. Unless of course, we are finally inspired, or forced by outside circumstances , or the IRS to devote all our attention to it.

The David and Goliath Game

Rather than doing the whole project at once, we can set the timer for just five or ten minutes, which turns the Big Project into a Little Project. I learned this trick a number of years back.

My wife and I had the typical great American garage—a garage so full that the car stayed in the driveway. We had good excuses of course—both our kids had moved out, and then moved back and then out again, leaving lots of their old and new stuff behind each time.

And both my mom and mother-in-law had recently passed on and much of their "mother stuff" also ended up stored in our garage. And then, come to find out, my wife and I also had plenty of our own "extra" stuff stored there. The garage had taken years to get so stuffed. To clean it out, even just to the point of being able to get the car in. was a huge project.

So one day I set the timer for five minutes to work on the garage. In that first five minutes I pounded in a nail to hang up the dust pan and another nail right above that for the whisk broom. There. Done. And it was kinda fun. I felt accomplished.

The next evening I gave myself ten minutes. And that, too, was fun. And then within a week or so —- bold man that I am—I started giving myself 30 minutes. We now park in the garage, and my tools are nicely hung up, and we have shelves. It's organized (sort of.)! My wife and I now do the same thing with taxes, and cleaning out the flower beds, and the storage room.

Here's why "short stints on huge projects" works! Often, when we begin to tackle these types of huge projects, we mistakenly, foolishly, subconsciously assume we'll work on it until "it's done." We set ourselves an almost impossible task unless we give ourselves, like my friend did, a full day to clean out a single drawer in the den.

When blindly we set out to tackle our Huge Projects, generally **the only reason we stop is because we run out of time or get frustrated, don't know where to put things, or find things. Or we get tired or called away to do something else**.

Thus, when we *next* think about going back to that Huge Project, we remember running out of time, or getting frustrated or tired, or interrupted. It's only natural that we don't want to go there again. THE FRAME IS AN UNCOMFORTABLE FRAME!

But when we think about the project—cleaning the garage or doing the taxes or cleaning out the closet— **and frame our attention** with, "I can do ten minutes worth," **we have a very-doable beginning and an end, a comfortable frame**. Then doing the project becomes easy.

The David and Goliath Game

When we devote five or ten or thirty or sixty minutes at a time, (using the timer, not the clock!) we don't get so tired or frustrated. **We aren't committed to working on the Huge Project until it's done. We most often don't have the time or energy or motivation for such a commitment**. But committing to such projects in short stints is, in fact, kinda fun!

Yes, of course, we aren't taught to work in this way. We are "supposed" to be disciplined enough to tackle huge projects and get them done all at once. And some people, even we ourselves on occasion, are indeed able to work this way. Most of us, however, most of the time, are not always so disciplined, or don't have such huge blocks of time or such motivation.

The timer, set for five or twenty or sixty minutes— works wonders for "Huge Projects." It lets us do what we need to do, peaceably, if not joyfully. And more important, **the timer allows us to get started**. As the Taoists say, *the journey of a thousand miles begins with a single step."*

Again, there are no rigid rules with this. Of course you can tackle Big Projects all at once— give yourself a full day, or a week or a month of dedicated attention to your project. That's one way of doing it. As the kids would say, go ahead, knock yourself out.

A somewhat more peaceable, and, for me at least, more consistently workable approach is t do it bit by bit, five, ten, twenty minutes at a time. As the old saying goes, "*How do you eat an entire elephant?*"

One bite at a time.

(P.S. That's also how you can read and apply this book!)

CHAPTER 4.

MOVE THE BOULDER GAME

Game 2: Using the timer for "one time" projects.

The task that interferes with your task <u>is</u> your task.
>   ----Buddhist saying

"Pleasure in the job puts perfection in the work."
>   --- Aristotle

*M*y wife and I recently installed a new, shiny light fixture over our dining room table. My own talents and interests would more likely lead me to *write a poem* about such a project rather than actually do it.

Nevertheless, installing a new light fixture is something we wanted to do, it needed to be done, so I set the timer for 90 minutes. Again, not that I was trying to get the deal done in 90 minutes. I set the timer so I would be more patient, more at rest with the inevitable "hang ups" (so to speak) that come with hanging and wiring a new light fixture.

As mentioned previously, experts suggest that **stress comes not so much from what we are doing, but from being interrupted in what we are doing.** When we take on a project such as hanging a chandelier, the "end result"—a newly hung chandelier—too easily becomes the image for "what we are doing."

Therefore, the stubbornness of the threads on the old light fixture to release their thirty-year grip might easily be viewed (especially for a poet such as myself) as an *interruption* of the light hanging project. My experience is that when I set the timer, what would have once been an *interruption* is now simply part of the process, i.e., part of the 90 minutes. I don't get so stressed or so cranky so easily. It's as if I've "scheduled time" to deal with the corroded threads on the old fixture. In other words, I better maintain my peace, my joy.

And this, let us remember is the reason we are playing with the timer in the first place: **to better maintain and enhance our experience of peace and joy in our everyday lives.** We play with the timer to have more fun, to more deeply experience the richness, the fullness, the immediacy of our lives.

Yes, we might find that by playing with the timer we get more things done, we are better organized, we are more persistent in working toward our goals. But these benefits are the gravy of the process. Increased joy and peace are the meat and potatoes.

If we should find times and places where the timer is getting in the way of our peace and joy, what do we do? We quickly abandon it! **If it's not fun, let's don't do it.**

Nevertheless, by "framing" our activities with the timer—ninety minutes to hang the new chandelier, for example—we are more likely to stay present, focused, in the flow. The old fixture in the ceiling that needs extra attention to remove is simply part of the "framework" that we put in place ahead of time. (Time!)

The "Move the Boulder" Game is for those one-time projects that need to be done, or at least call to be done, and most often can and should be done in a single effort. (Like hanging the chandelier, or fixing the oven light, though that one—fixing the oven light—actually took me several weeks, but that's another story.)

The "boulder" doesn't have to be huge. Ninety-minute huge is my preferred huge. Of course, sometimes we need to devote two or three hours, or a whole day, even a week to a project. But the timer isn't as useful for these projects. However, having trained one's self with the timer to be more patient, more peaceable, more in the moment, comes in quite handy.

In the past week or two I have used the "move the boulder" Timer Game to mend a wobbly gate post, to get an old wall clock to once again tell the right time, to stop the ice maker from making too much ice (that one will need some more attention), and to experiment with the "hot water method" of removing weeds from the Zen garden. (That, too, will need more attention.)

Obviously, we don't want to or need to set the timer for everything we do during the day. That would be neither fun nor practical. But when some particular project needs attention—some boulder in the road that perhaps has been there for a while but we keep walking around, planning to "move it later"—I find the little kitchen timer is a great "assistant" to help move such boulders more easily, in a more (dare I say it) timely fashion?

This is not rocket science. Once I suggest how to use the timer in this way to make a project easier, it becomes obvious, "of course." Nevertheless, sometimes it's nice to remind each other of these "obvious" easier ways.

Before we leave this chapter, here are two more time quotes I had wanted to use but couldn't find the right place for. So here they are, on their own, just for fun:

Move the Boulder Game

"*Time is the coin of your life. It is the only coin you have, and only you can determine how it will be spent. Be careful lest you let other people spend it for you.* - Carl Sandburg

"*Work is love made visible. And if you cannot work with love but only with distaste, it is better that you should leave your work and sit at the gate of the temple and take alms of those who work with joy.*"   ---Kahlil Gibran

CHAPTER 5.

FILL IN THE BLANK GAME

GAME 3: I HAVE A LITTLE TIME BEFORE I GO.... "

"A double minded man is unstable in all his ways." – James 1;8

*I*t's 3:00 p.m., and I've agreed to meet cousin Louie at the hardware store at 4:00 p.m. so he can help me pick out which faucet works best for our basement bathroom. It will take me ten minutes to get there, and five minutes to park, so what do I do for the next forty-five minutes? A load of laundry? Read a book? Check my e-mail? Work more on the basement bathroom? Do I do nothing, or something? How do I decide what to do? Or not do?

Obviously, this is not a life or death circumstance, and I've got lots of wiggle room. But situations such as this rise up all the time! And time is what we're working with here!

From past experience, I know that if I *don't* use my timer, what I WILL do for the next forty-five minutes is check the damned clock, every five or ten minutes.

And in doing so I'll be working in a "double-minded" way, which as James suggests, makes me "unstable in all my ways."

What is unstable? My peace of mind!

"Clock watching" itself can be somewhat irritating, or at least bothersome, **because my attention, whatever it's on, is continually being interrupted!** Each time I check the clock I'm obliged to decide once again if I have enough time to keep doing what I'm doing, or do nothing, or ...?

Like most people, I often try to accomplish too many things "before going"—whether going off to work in the morning or to a party in the evening or to a meeting in the mid-afternoon. Either that, or I don't accomplish anything, because, obviously, "there's not enough time." 'When I need to leave in twenty minutes, I either don't get started on anything (not enough time) or try to do too much.

I've learned that if I set my timer, I can decide *just once*, what I have time to do, whether it's read a book or clean out a drawer or check my e-mail When I make the decision to do something for "ten minutes," (or twenty or five, depending on departure time) and then set the timer, **I don't have to think about it again.** My timer allows for a smooth transition between "here and there," and leads to a rather low-level, yet nevertheless enjoyable, productivity.

Using a timer to help get me out of the house, or out of the office or out of the yard, on time is like having a personal assistant, or stage manager, who schedules what I am doing during the day, watches the time for me and makes sure I am where I am supposed to be, when I'm supposed to be there.

Again, it's not the key to salvation, but using the timer to "frame" the hours or minutes I have before needing to leave is a simple little "trick"—or life hack—that consistently allows me to more easily, more gracefully relax a little, be in the present, stay in the flow, indeed, *establish* a flow. The real benefit of this trick is that, rather than thinking, worrying about meeting cousin Louie an hour from now, **I'm able to rest my attention of whatever I'm doing in the present moment**! Getting more things done with less effort is just a happy side benefit!

CHAPTER 6
THE *HAPPY LITTLE COG* GAME

GAME # 4 : TWENTY MINUTE "CALL THE CABLE COMPANY" OR OTHER INSTITUTION

"Bureaucracy is a giant mechanism operated by pygmies."
--- Honore de Balzac

*A*t one time I thought I could set my timer to make it easier to call Uncle Waldo—which I often hesitated to do because Uncle Waldo, living by himself, can get real talky, go on and on and on. But I discovered that setting a timer for such personal calls doesn't work. It feels mean and artificial and shallow. **It seems that for people we know and love, or for colleagues, friends and neighbors, the timer can get in the way**.

To me, it feels fake, unnatural to "frame" our relationships in this way. When I try to put another live human being that I know and care about into my "timer frame," the human gets squished. We humans don't fit into frames like that. (If you figure out a way to do that, let me know!)

Nevertheless, using the timer *does* work to make things easier, more peaceable when calling the phone company, or the bank or insurance people, or the doctor's office or the stockbroker, any of those institutions where, after dialing, we are connected with a friendly lady robot, (why is it always a lady?) and then, following her instructions, putting in our account number or pushing 1, 2 or 3 to let her know what we're calling about, we finally hear, "*Your call is important to us. Please stay on the line.*"

It used to be that our calls were truly so important to these big institutions that they actually had real people answer their phones. (L.L. Bean still has real people answer their phones, from the first! No wonder they stay successful.)

I have learned that when I have some business I must do over the phone with one of these large institutions, in which I function as one of their "outside cogs" and I will be talking to an "inside cog," if I set my timer for fifteen or twenty minutes—however long I think it might take, and then, based on past experience, add a few more minutes—the robot lady is not such a pest. With my timer, I've already accounted for her. (She is no longer an *interruption*!) And when I get switched from one "service representative," e.g. "service cog, " to another, it's not such an interruption, such an inconvenience. I've already accounted for it, by setting my timer. Again, **_stress,_ researchers tell us, does not come from what we are _doing_, but from being _interrupted_ in what we are doing**.

Not that we're going to hang up or cut them off after fifteen minutes if our business isn't taken care of by that time. But setting the timer helps us put the task into a framework, and we can more easily see how it fits in the day. For this same reason, I also often use my timer when filling out online applications, or making online queries about some product or service.

Again, like most folks, I tend to either over-estimate or underestimate the amount of time it takes for these affairs. The advantage of using the timer here is that **we bring our inner estimate to the outer mechanism—the timer—and somehow the task becomes more peaceable, and thus more do-able**. Timing such outreaching may seem a silly, unnecessary addendum to our day—and sometimes it is. But again, test it out. You will be surprised at how much peace this little timer can bring to talking with your cell phone service provider!

CHAPTER 7
THE **HOLD YOUR NOSE AND DO IT** GAME

GAME 5: THE FIFTEEN MINUTE *"HATE TO DO IT/ HAVE TO DO IT "* PROJECT FRAMES

"The robbed that smiles, steals something from the thief."
                                        ---Shakespeare (Othello)

*W*e all have regular tasks we'd rather not do but we hold our nose and do them anyway.

The bills do have to be paid, the dog has to be walked, and washed. The kitchen cleaned up! Putting the timer to such tasks allows us to see beyond the tasks—-to see where in our day, or morning or evening—- these "smelly" tasks will fit.

Obviously, I say "fifteen minutes" but these can be ten or twenty-minute time frames. Again, the timer helps us to be in the moment, in the flow, not resisting our lives and the delicious (though sometimes smelly) "daily duties" that in fact are the meat and potatoes of living the good life, here on earth.

Using the timer for "*hate to do it, have to do it*" projects is somewhat akin to using the timer to start "Big Projects" or for calling the Cell Phone Company, but here we're putting attention on the more mundane, everyday tasks.

As mentioned, my wife and I have learned to use the timer to prepare our taxes—which for us is one of those "*hate to do it/have to do it*" chores. Some people, I understand, love to do their taxes (though I don't really understand). For example, we have a friend, Charlotte, who has trained herself to keep such good tax records throughout the year that she files her taxes on **January 3rd** every year! She owns her own business, and is apparently happy and willing to spend six, seven or eight hours all in one shot filling out all the forms, crossing the t's and dotting the I's, getting straight with Uncle Sam. She's proud to be a "first responder" when it comes to takes.

I, on the other hand, seem to have a mental and emotional block when it comes to doing, and paying, taxes. Maybe it comes, in part, from knowing that our latest B-21 bomber had development costs of $23 *billion* and even after such development each bomber costs over $*600 million* to produce. As a monk, I'm not big on bombers. My basic, and long–standing, plea to our government is, "Please, let's stop bombing people."

48

Hold Your Nose and Do It Game

(Saw a great bumper sticker recently: "When Jesus said, *Love Your Enemies*, I think he meant, *don't kill them*.")

Nevertheless, even being a monk at Heart Mountain Monastery, I still pay my taxes. But I do have this mental and emotional block that I know I should probably just get over. And I am getting over it, if ever so slowly, with the help of my timer.

Still, every year for past thirty years or more, on April fourteenth or so, I've filed for the automatic extension. Such differences—between my approach and Charlotte's approach— are what make the world go around!

Thus, I generally start to think about doing my taxes sometime in August or September. (The "automatic extension" means my tax returns aren't due until October 15th). With the pressure of the looming deadline, at some point on some day a month or two before the deadline I set my timer for fifteen minutes to deal with this "hate to do it/have to do it" chore of tax preparation. Fifteen minutes? What can I get done in fifteen minutes?

Not much.

But it eases my brain to know I WILL be done in just fifteen minutes. That in itself is useful. I won't get done with the whole tax return of course, but I'll get done, at least for today, with this "hate to do it/have to do it" chore. So, knowing fifteen minutes worth of tax stuff probably won't kill me, I give myself permission to proceed.

Actually, it's quite surprising what can be accomplished in just fifteen minutes—gathering papers, or looking for papers. Looking at bank statements, etc. When the timer goes off after fifteen minutes, I can put the whole stack away again. "That was easy, and productive!" The next night, it's easier. I *almost* look forward to doing it again. And then the night after that. At just fifteen, or even twenty minutes at a time, come to find out doing taxes can be kinda fun!

Of course, this approach to doing taxes would drive some people, like Charlotte, nuts! For my wife and me, it works just fine.

But there are other *"hate to do it, have to do it"* chores: Cleaning closets or drawers, sorting laundry, organizing the garage, mowing the lawn, compiling monthly reports. All these become much easier chores when they have a time frame, a timer frame around them.

Again, the principle here is that, with chores and projects that we *"hate to do, but have to do,"* **when we frame our attention with the timer, attention stays willingly more focused, and thus flows smoother.**

Hold Your Nose and Do It Game

When our attention flows smoother, *our lives flow smoother!* Is there a better reason than this for using the timer?

Chapter 8.

The Daily Bus Schedule Game
Game 6: Time Your Routine Chores

"Time is an illusion. Lunch time doubly so."
                            --- Douglas Adams

*I*t's comforting to know that the bus will arrive at the same time every day, and we can either catch it or not.

Same thing with regular chores: It's nice to know they will probably take the same amount of time every day, whether we do them or not. So it's useful to time these regular chores, at least once or twice, to see how long they actually do take!

This is a little different use for the timer. In previous "uses," we were absolutely NOT trying to "get done"—doing the dishes or cleaning a drawer or mowing the lawn— in a certain fixed amount of time (unless that's a fun little game you want to play.)

To repeat: We set the timer, **not** to try to "get it done" in a particular amount of time, but rather simply to *allow* ourselves that time, *give* ourselves that time to do just that, whatever we are doing— the dishes, or the drawer or the lawn.

Most often when using the timer, we're not focused on the *quantity* of time we are devoting to a given project, but rather the *quality* of time we are giving. It's what makes the timer such a valuable, uplifting little buddy, sidekick.

Here, however, we are simply curious about how much time it takes to actually do a particular chore. Again, we're not trying to do it in a particular amount of time. We're just curious about *how much* time it *naturally* takes.

For example, we have two bird feeders on the back porch, and one out by the dining room window. Anybody who has bird feeders knows it's a fun idea to begin with, but the feeders do need to be refilled on a regular basis.

I confess, several months after installing our feeders I started to feel a bit burdened by this repetitive chore. (Those little bird brains kept emptying the feeder—with a little help from their squirrel buddies.)

One morning I set my timer, assuming filling the feeders was about a ten-minute chore. Come to find out it took me less than three minutes! I was *very* surprised.

I had been making it a much bigger chore in my head than it was in real life. Isn't this true for many of our chores? Knowing it takes less than three minutes, I now find it easy to refill the feeders.

Curiously, in the same way, it takes only a little more than four minutes to unload the dishwasher. That's a chore we make bigger in our head than it actually is in real life. And the same goes for sorting the laundry and cleaning the bathroom. Reading and answering e-mail, on the other hand, generally takes much *longer* than we expect.

Obviously, this is a little different from setting the timer to allow attention to rest on a particular chore, where we aren't concerned about how much time it takes to accomplish the chore. Here we want to know how long it actually takes to **do** a chore. Timing these small chores just once or twice is generally enough to release the false sense of time.

Other examples:

Making the bed: Two minutes (or less.) Don't believe me? Just time it!

Watering the plants, depending on the locations and number of your plants, and *how* you water, of course: Forty-five minutes. (Much LONGER than I generally assume it will take. But I'm a bonsai nut.)

Sorting and loading laundry into washing machine: Seven minutes (doesn't it always feel like it takes much longer?)

Folding and putting laundry away: Three days (to get to it.) Less than fifteen minutes to actually do it!

Vacuuming the living room rug: Two weeks (sometimes) to get to it; ten minutes for a "lick and promise" approach which makes it *look* 98% better; twenty minutes if you want to move furniture, get under the table, etc. etc. Then it *feels* 100% better.

A shower: I can get it done in under five minutes (depending on when I start timing) but I much prefer twenty minutes, or until just *before* the hot water runs out.

Mowing the lawn: Forty minutes (depending, of course, on the lawn.)

Why are we doing this—timing our chores? For fun. And because we're curious. And to make our future days go smoother, to enjoy our present days more, be more at peace with our day. This is after all, as we learned in the introduction, the most important thing for ourselves and all those around us!

Chapter 9
The "Aunt Mary's Coming!" Game
Game 7: Ten minute "clean-up, pick-up" frames

"There is no daily chore so trivial that it cannot be made important by skipping it two days running."

---- Robert Brault

*S*o Aunt Mary calls and says she and Uncle Howard just happen to be in town on their way to a goat show and they'd like to come by to say hello and bring you an apple pie she baked.

"Oh great, " you say. "We'd love to see you."

"We'll be there in about ten minutes," Aunt Mary says.

"Wonderful," you say, and then when you hang up the phone, "Oh my God! Bruce!" You yell to your hubby. "Aunt Mary and Uncle Howard will be here in ten minutes."

Amazing, isn't it, how clean, or at least how much cleaner, the house can get in ten minutes when company is on the way?

Just because we live in them, our homes get messy. And just because we work there, our offices get chaotic.

At home, on a regular basis, the living room needs picked up, the bathroom cleaned, the laundry folded and put away. At the office, paper detritus collects, memos pile up, reports get stacked.

We can expect to be faced with "tidying" chores until we're carted off to the nursing home!

Even then, however, research shows that if we have little chores—just watering our little plant on our nursing home window—we'll feel better, have a quicker healing time, stay healthier.

I have learned that when I (at least on occasion) give my routine chores a "time frame," by setting my timer, I enjoy the chores more! And thus I get more chores done.

Somehow, it's a lot easier for me to get started on "ten minutes to pick up the living room," then just start on picking up the living room. Whether it's five minutes, ten minutes, twenty or thirty, **deciding on the time frame is the key to *flow***.

Aunt Mary's Coming! Game

We can *pretend* that Aunt Mary is coming in ten minutes!

My wife would often do this with our kids when they were young. "We're going to clean your room for five minutes." And she would set the timer. It was a game and they enjoyed it, once they actually got into it. They knew there was an end to this chore.

And again, it's amazing how much cleaning can get done in just five minutes!

We're all kids at heart, yes? Let's play more games, as we clean things up.

CHAPTER 10.

THE *LET'S GET BUFF* GAME

GAME 8 : USING THE TIMER FOR PHYSICAL EXERCISES

"I don't exercise. If God wanted me to bend over he'd have put diamonds on the floor." --- Joan Rivers

*O*ne of the most common uses for a timer is in relation to doing physical exercises. "Sports watches" come with built in timers—and heart rate monitors and step counters and brain scans—- for this exact reason

Lots of folks already have a physical routine that they have "timed," either intentionally or not. When my neighbor says he's going to the gym, (I ask him to do a few reps for me while he's there), he generally knows how long he will be there. He might make it a short day or a long day, but he has an inner "time frame" for his workout.

Some yoga practitioners, to increase the intensity and/or depth of their practice, will employ a timer and "hold" a stretch, or a particular asana, for a specific amount of time. When two minutes might seem like forever at the beginning of the month, by the end of the month—or even the end of the week—two minutes flies by (like a downward facing dog?).

Rather than timing particular exercises—a fairly advanced and "serious" use of the timer— we might use it simply to give ourselves a clear and simple framework of ten or twenty minutes of stretching, or breathing exercises, or weight lifting, whatever. Again, it's much easier, more relaxing and efficient to use a timer rather than a clock.

For example, if I decide I want to walk for thirty minutes, especially if I'm in a new setting, I'll set my timer for fifteen minutes and head out the door. When the timer rings, I know it's time to turn back.

Around our own homes, of course, most of us know our regular "walking routes" and how much time each route normally takes. The timer isn't quite so necessary or useful in these well-known situations.

But when we travel, visiting different cities or exploring new parts of the world, even simply staying at a new motel, the timer is a handy framing device.

When our son and his wife lived in Austin, I explored the neighborhoods around their home on successive days simply by walking thirty minutes in each direction. It was a wonderful way of gaining a perspective of his neighborhood. Again, putting a "frame" around such explorations encourages these explorations, makes them more easily engaged.

Of course, many physical exercises, such as sit-ups or push-ups or pumping iron, or jogging, have their own "built in" timer—e.g., how many reps you decide to do, or how far do you plan to jog. Timers are not quite as useful in these areas, though they are useful for timing an overall session. No clock watching!

As the old saying goes, "The best exercise is the one you will do." I find my timer does help me to actually *do* physical exercise.

Again, I sometimes think about how good it would be for me, and maybe even fun, if I went to shoot some hoops in the small park across the street. Alas, I seldom actually do it. *Unless,* I tell myself, "okay, I'm going to give myself fifteen minutes for shooting hoops." Such a frame somehow helps get me off the couch, or away from the computer, and out into the fresh air.

In the end, this little five-dollar timer helps us to become more physically fit. What a bargain!

CHAPTER 11.
THE "RODIN'S THINKER" GAME

Game # 9: Use the timer to "Think About That"

"No problem can withstand the assault of sustained thinking." --- Voltaire

"You have to allow a certain amount of time in which you are doing nothing in order to have things occur to you, to let your mind think." --- Mortimer Adler

*W*e obviously spend much time thinking about many, many things that are very important to us, or just interesting to us—our work, our kids, our parents, our future, our homes—but we generally do such thinking in brief, random, **one and two second fits, flashes, jumbled smorgasbords.**

If it is a problem that is important to us, thinking with these fits and flashes and jumbled musings might repeat again and again throughout the day, but still, we seldom devote specific, prolonged time to considering the situation.

To give ourselves five minutes—timed with a timer—to think about one particular topic proves to be very powerful. We can often get more "thinking" done in five dedicated minutes than in a week of random musings. Five minutes dedicated to thinking about one thing can lead to brilliance!

When I have something I want to think more deeply about, maybe even while I'm out walking, I'll set my timer. When my thoughts wander, as they inevitably do, I simply and gently bring them back to the topic at hand. Again, we can become addicted to this process because it often leads to *very* powerful insights.

A subtle linguistic point: As we have discussed in earlier chapters, when we set the timer to think about a particular topic for a particular amount of time, which is regularly done in school, in business focus groups and in psychotherapy, we aren't actually *thinking* about this topic. In fact, **we are suspending our habitual thinking patterns in order to put our *attention* on this topic. *Attention is prior to thinking. Attention generates thinking.***

It's a subtle point, but useful. "Let me think about that," actually means, "Let me put my attention on that for a minute." It's our *attention* that's powerful!

Attention leads to insights. When we set the timer to put our attention on something for a specified amount of time, we discover its secrets!

Creativity = Compress, Then Release

At a conference some years ago, I heard the controversial and somewhat wacky Dr. Patrick Flanagan, describe his creative process. He suggested his was THE creative process behind most scientific breakthroughs.

(Somewhat wacky, for instance, in that during his lecture he demonstrated a part of his high school gymnastics routine by doing a back flip and then a quite impressive parallel balance using the back of a chair.)

In its September 14th, 1962 issue, *Life Magazine* tagged him as a "whiz kid" and one of the ten top young scientists in the country. One of Dr. Flanagan's inventions, which he brought out before he was 16 years old, was a fairly simple device which could detect the launching of a guided missile thousands of miles away. He sold it the U.S. Army. Years later he quit his work with the U.S. Navy, where he was helping to compile a dictionary of dolphin language, when he discovered they were planning to use their dolphins to deliver torpedoes. His latest work focuses on revolutionary ways to help the body absorb essential nutrients.

So, Dr. Flanagan's take on the creative process: First, he said, one must clearly articulate the problem one is trying to solve, and then over hours, weeks, months or years, put all one's energy (all one's *attention*!) into it. Work hard, he said, think hard, and then work hard some more and then think hard some more to find the solution. Put everything you have, mentally, emotionally and physically, into solving the problem, just *push, push, push,* take it as far as you can take it, out to the very edge, mentally, emotionally, physically.

This doesn't seem very "insightful" or new. It's what we're encouraged to do from grade school. But here was Dr. Flanagan's insight:

At the end point where you can't give it any more—be it for the day or the week or the year—when you have nothing left to give . . .

Let go. Release. Take a shower. Go for a swim. Make a pan of lasagna. Take a vacation. Go to the Bahamas.

He said, "Ninety percent of the time it is after you let go of the hard effort, when you're making the lasagna, or in the shower, after you've given it everything, and you're no longer thinking about it. No longer pushing, the real and elegant solution to the problem pops out." (Dr. Flanagan words are being paraphrased here.)

The Rodin Thinker Buff Game

On a humbler, more down to earth (and quicker) level, the use of the timer to "think about it" for five minutes or so mimics this very powerful process. By concentrating on a problem, large or small, for a set number of minutes, we mimic the *"push, push push—then let go"* creative process. We get the subconscious cooking.

For a very mundane example: maybe we're unhappy with the way our back yard "flows"—or doesn't flow—when we have folks over for a garden party. We probably think about how to organize our back yard landscaping off and on for months, or even years.   We'll get an idea here or there, especially when we're glancing through a magazine or visiting gardens in England, whatever.

The suggestion here is to use the timer and **JUST THINK ABOUT THE BACKYARD LANDSCAPING (or whatever)   FOR FIVE STRAIGHT DEDICATED MINUTES**.

Of course, the nature of the mind is that it's going to wander   even during those "five dedicated minutes." So be it. The suggestion here is to simply guide the mind—or more accurately, the attention—back to the backyard landscaping, or whatever problem you have chosen.

Five minutes of dedicated "let me think about that" is often more actual "_time_" spent on the problem than months of momentary, random musings when the project is on the "back burner."

I have found that with these dedicated five minutes (I rarely have the mind power to take it beyond five minutes), I often come up with great new insights. Or if not *great,* than at least adequate, and clever little solutions to various problems in the course of my five-minute thinking exercise.

However, the surprising "bonus prize" for doing this five-minute *"let me think about that"* exercise is that it sets the subconscious mind working on the problem in ways that it hasn't done before. Once I give five *dedicated* minutes to thinking about a problem—sometimes five minutes numerous times over days or weeks—I have time and again found elegant, often quite surprising solutions to problems large and small popping up out of nowhere during my "off times," e.g. when I am making lasagna, or playing with the dog, no longer thinking about that specific problem or relationship.

The five minute *"let me think about that"* game works with both the conscious and the subconscious mind in ways that we don't generally engage, at least on the conscious level.

In fact, though, we actually do follow this "*push, push, push, then relax*" procedure quite often, because it's the way we humans often get things done here on earth. When we *consciously* engage the procedure, we are showing our maturity! Or maybe just our quirkiness.

In the next chapter we'll take a deeper look at two other ways that that the timer can, like the five-minute *let-me-think-about that* game, help us "integrate" the conscious and subconscious mind, for both personal and communal advantage. It is not surprising that "concentrated thinking, with relaxation," are also the fundamental processes underlining meditation and prayer

Which is what we'll talk in the next chapter.

Chapter 12.
The "Beam Me Up, Scotty!" Game
Game # 10: Using the Timer for Prayer and Meditation

Joy is prayer; joy is strength; joy is love; joy is a net of love by which you can catch souls. --- Mother Teresa

*I*t's tough to be happy for five minutes straight. But worth the effort!

A couple of monk buddies and I sometimes play a game during our weekly gathering where we set the timer for five minutes to challenge ourselves to simply *enjoy* everything that comes up, within or without.

The challenge is to enjoy all of our thoughts, all of our sensations, each of the sounds in the room, the traffic going by. We are even challenged to enjoy the inner response that says, "This is goofy." Such an exercise quickly shows us our habitual crankiness.

Like I said, it's tough to be happy for five minutes straight. But worth the effort.

Such an exercise shows us it's possible to *intentionally,* consciously enjoy our lives a little more than we do. Again, **enjoying our lives a little more is what the timer is all about**.

I love using my timer for these types of mental and emotional games and experiments. For me, consciously enjoying life and what it has to offer in each moment is one form of prayer—one form of meditation—and one of its simplest forms, one of the main reasons we pray and meditate.

In a variation of the above five-minute exercise (prayer, or meditation), when I coach people stopping smoking, one of the exercises I regularly share is to set the timer for just one minute. I tell my client, "**okay for one minute, we're just going to love. Love your thoughts, love your feelings, love your judgments, love your fears, whatever comes up. Just love it. Even love your antagonistic feelings about your goofy counselor**".

Many clients told me that this simple little *"one minute love"* exercise—when they took it with them and occasionally did it on their own—helped them quit smoking more than anything else they had done.

(People find it easier to stop smoking when they feel good about themselves and want to feel still better rather than when they beat themselves up all the time.)

Such is the healing power of prayer, even simple, accidental, "unknowing" prayer. Most of my clients were not aware that "just loving everything that comes up" is a form of prayer!

Use the Timer for Traditional Prayer and Meditation

"Those not busy being born are busy dying."
—Bob Dylan

Even the most agnostic or atheistic "self-help" experts suggest starting the day with some form of mental discipline—whether reviewing one's goals for getting rich or pumping one's self up for another day at the circus.

Every spiritual tradition suggests the same thing: it's very useful, for mental, emotional and physical health, to **start the day by tuning in to the wider presence (Presence)—the wider life (Life) that is the basis of What Is Going On (WIGO)** both within and without.

As a householder monk at Heart Mountain Monastery I start (most) every day with at least a little bit of enjoyable (rather than arduous) prayer and meditation. And, yes, I use my timer.

Over the years, the actual methods (I'm a Buddhist *Methodist*, after all) and forms of this morning "tuning in" have naturally changed, evolved. I have had seasons where for several hours I would pray, meditate and/or study (study scripture, and scriptural books, which is another form of praying and meditating).

I've had other seasons, days, where a minute or two is all I had, or wanted. So sue me.

Curiously, over the years, the evolution of my practice has been mostly toward "simplifying," rather than getting more and more complex. I have had wonderful seasons where I would use the timer for set periods of time—one minute, five minutes, seven minutes—to engage particular prayers, particular meditations, one after another.

I've had other seasons where I *didn't* use the timer, but just trusted my own intuition and inspiration about what was enough. Alas, I've found my "intuition and inspiration" is hard to separate from my impatience and personal ambition. In other words, without the timer I'd often end my periods of prayer and meditation because I was getting antsy rather than inspired!

My current morning prayer and meditation session (most days) is divided between three periods, using slightly different methods in each. The first period is twenty minutes, where I engage in fairly formal prayer and meditation "techniques," as taught by both Western and Eastern traditions.

The "Beam Me Up, Scotty," Game

The second period is seven minutes—an "eyes open" meditation very similar to the "one minute enjoy" or "one minute just love" meditation.

And then a final three minutes of direct, intense tuning, listening, praying, communicating.

Thus, it's a total of thirty-one minutes. More than some. Much less than others. No praise, no blame.

As the Jehovah's Witnesses are fond of saying, "*If you can count the number of times a day you pray, you aren't praying enough.*"

The morning prayer and meditation time is the "foundation" for a day of prayer and meditation. "Rejoice always, pray without ceasing," suggested St. Paul to the Thessalonians.

Except for a few easy, mostly traditional prayers while in bed before going to sleep, I confess, in this season of my life I don't have formal "evening" prayer and meditation times, though in other seasons I did indeed make time for such devotions. I do feel myself moving in that direction again, but as of this writing, it just ain't happening.

Which doesn't mean I don't pray and meditate in the evening hours—mostly with study of inspiring books, and/or brief one word prayers and meditations appropriate for the moment. I spend most evenings with my wife and friends, enjoying "good company," known as "*satsang*" in the east.

The exact form or method of your prayer and/or meditation—be it formal or informal—is not as important as the actual **willingness to engage**, especially on a regular basis. The universe is very understanding, and very forgiving. It knows what you want to do—open to deeper rhythms, hear deeper meaning, be at peace with the wider forces. So just start doing it—and you will be guided, led to do it the way that's exactly right for you.

Boring, Boring, Boring

Most friends and clients with whom I've talked about this often report that they "tried" prayer and/or meditation but for one reason or another gave it up. When I inquire about the details, I find that they were mostly following very traditional methods, doing it the way they were "supposed to" or had been taught to do it. And of course, this is appropriate for beginners.

But with the same "warning" that I started this little book, when it comes to prayer and meditation, **if it's not fun, don't do it**! As blasphemous as it sounds, this the key that we are given in order to enter and explore the higher dimensions: make it fun, make it interesting, make it personal!

The "Beam Me Up, Scotty," Game

If it's not fun, find a way to *make it* fun. Contacting the divine, contacting the Buddha mind, contacting the Deeper Reality is contacting joy, contacting peace, inspiration, aliveness! If you don't *feel* the contact, experience the contact, even a whisper of it, then it might be best to try a different door! **What we are looking for in prayer and meditation—the sign that we are successful—is the "spontaneous grin,"** the grin, the release, that pops up on its own, even if only for a second, due to something that has arisen within. We don't need any more empty ritual, hoping for bennies "later." We want the grin right now!

Yes, there are traditions—especially from the East, but also in many Jewish and Christian sects—that suggest we need to "suffer through" our boredom with our meditation, our impatience, our seeming lack of progress. I'll let them argue their own reasons for this.

But what kind of friend would you rather have: one who is easy and fun to be with, whom you look forward to seeing again because he or she always surprises you and makes you laugh , or a friend who is somewhat rigid, tough and in fact quite boring though demanding of your time?

Prayer and meditation can become your friends—your best friends, your daily companions. They will continue to change, just as you do. Make it a fun journey with them.

They'll be with you, even after you drop the body. Now THAT is a friendship with nourishing, yes?

CHAPTER 13.

THE *NO-GAMES* GAME

Game 11: One Minute "Letting Go'" meditations

"How beautiful it is to do nothing and then to rest afterwards." – Spanish proverb

*T*his final, quick game, sort of like the cherry on top of the sundae, is easy, at least on the surface. But to "perfect" this game takes a lifetime.

Here it is: Simply set the timer for one minute, and **do nothing**!

For one minute allow yourself to *not* fix any problems, yours or others. Just rest, be at peace, enjoy all the thoughts inside, all the sights outside, all the relationships and lack of relationships. **Do nothing for just one minute.**

Just breathe. For just one minute, just be! For many beginners in this game it may help or be useful to use a word or phrase to remind yourself what you're doing here. Simply, "let go," or "just enjoy," or "just be" or, one of my favorites, *"no problem solving."* When you find your attention getting caught on some inner or outer story or condition, or problem to solve, return to your phrase, "let go."

To give yourself one lousy minute where you're not solving problems is okay! In fact, it's healthy, refreshing, rejuvenating.

After your one minute of "letting go," if you feel so moved, you are free to do another minute, and then another. You can do these one minute "let go" meditations anywhere— in the car, or walking, or at work. I have no doubt you will find such a practice very, very refreshing— uplifting!

When working with addictions I have found that this one-minute "let go" exercise is powerful. (After all, walking away from an addiction is just *letting it go*, yes?) Most of us are very addicted to being somewhere else in our heads, in the past or the future. This is a nice little game to bring us back to the now.

So what's your response to this last little Timer Game ? Let it go!

And here you are, with nothing to do.

CONCLUSION

"Baseball is ninety percent mental and the other half is physical." – Yogi Berra

"**S**etting the timer all the time would drive me crazy," my grown son Sam once told me, recognizing my continual use of the little gadget. I laughed and accepted his resistance.

It was the Christmas season, and we had some packages to mail. "This should take us about thirty minutes," I guessed, and set my timer.

When we walked into the post office, we saw the line stretched back to the door. "Oh no," my son said.

"It's okay, we have time," I said, showing him my timer. It had taken five minutes to drive to the post office. He grinned and shook his head.

"Sorry about the long line," the postal clerk said when we finally made it to the front desk.

"Not so bad," I said. "It took us about seventeen minutes." I showed him my timer. He laughed.

Again, **stress comes not so much from what you are doing as from being interrupted in what you are doing**. When our goal was to "mail Christmas packages," then the long line was an *interruption* in what we were doing. When we gave ourselves thirty minutes to mail the packages, then the long line was simply part of the process. Stress was reduced.

A while later, I noticed my son had set a timer next to his computer to complete some "work-from-home" assignments he had from his art studio.

Contrary to what it might first appear, playing these timer games is a simple, natural and easy way to *reduce* stress in our life.

Gloria Mark, professor in the Department of Informatics at the University of California, Irvine, studied office workers in high-tech firms, tracking activities and "interruptions" down to the second. Timing when a worker would pick up the phone, and then hang up.

In an interview with Kermit Pattison for *Fast Company* she said, "We had observers go into the workplace and we timed people's activities to the second. We've been to various workplaces, all high-tech companies. We wanted to look at information workers.

Conclusion

We had observers shadow each person for three and a half days each and timed every activity to the second. If they pick up a phone call, that's the start time. When they put the phone down, that's the stop time. When they turn to the Word application we get the start time and stop time. We found people switched these activities on average of every three minutes and five seconds.

"Roughly half of them are self-interruptions. That's to me an endless source of fascination: why do people self-interrupt? I do that all the time." (From Fast Company, July 28, 2008)

Might use of the timer be a way to *not* continually self-interrupt? I think the answer is obvious. Yes, of course that's exactly what we're doing!

The "Timer Games" that I have outlined in this little book are designed to make our daily lives more fun, more interesting, more peaceable. I would love to hear how *you* use the timer! (I'm a timer nut!)

Please send me your comments and suggestions.

And thanks for taking the time to read this little missive. May all your days be bright!

Bear Gebhardt

bear@heartmountainmonastery.com

ABOUT THE AUTHOR

Bear Jack Gebhardt is a "householder monk" at Heart Mountain Monastery, Nunnery and Art Colony, and the organizer of the New Buddhist Methodist Church, while still spending a bit of time as Head Coach at the Smokers Freedom School.

Bear is married to the artist, Suzy Summers Gebhardt. They have two grown children and two grandchildren. He spends most days putting his attention on what he loves, and encourages others to do the same. He loves to read, hike in the nearby mountains (both alone and with friends), tweak his stock portfolio, lunch and dine and play poker with both old and new friends and oh yea, as often as possible, do his part to foment non-violent revolution, striving to bring more political, economic and spiritual power back to ordinary people.

See Amazon author's page and/or:

www.beargebhardt.com

www.heartmountainmonastery.com

www.newmethodistchurch.com

Other Books by Bear Gebhardt

- *A Wave of Thanks: and Other Human Gestures: 31 Quick Stories*

- *The Smoker's Prayer: The Spiritual Healing of Tobacco Addiction, with or without Chantix, Nicotine Patches, Hypnosis, Jail Time or Duct Tape*

- *The Potless Pot High: How to Get High, Clear and Spunky without Weed*

- *How to Stop Smoking in 15 Easy Years: A Slacker's Guide to Final Freedom*

- *Practicing the Presence of Peace*

- *Happy John: An Advaita (Non-duality) Gospel*

- *How to Help Your Smoker Quit—A Brave and Happy Strategy*

- *The Enlightened Smoker's Guide To Quitting*

- *Now Hiring: Finding and Keeping Good Help for Your Entry Wage Jobs*   (With Steve Lauer)